T0120829

SHATTERED

Dealing with loss & depression

In light of the pandemic, Covid 19 Virus, the death toll rises daily. This is a timely book to help you navigate through loss as well as depression.

JEAN ANN DIBENEDETTO

WESTBOW
PRESS®
A DIVISION OF THOMAS NELSON
& ZONDERVAN

Copyright © 2021 Jean Ann DiBenedetto.

All rights reserved. No part of this book may be used or reproduced by any means, graphic, electronic, or mechanical, including photocopying, recording, taping or by any information storage retrieval system without the written permission of the author except in the case of brief quotations embodied in critical articles and reviews.

This book is a work of non-fiction. Unless otherwise noted, the author and the publisher make no explicit guarantees as to the accuracy of the information contained in this book and in some cases, names of people and places have been altered to protect their privacy.

WestBow Press books may be ordered through booksellers or by contacting:

WestBow Press
A Division of Thomas Nelson & Zondervan
1663 Liberty Drive
Bloomington, IN 47403
www.westbowpress.com
844-714-3454

Because of the dynamic nature of the Internet, any web addresses or links contained in this book may have changed since publication and may no longer be valid. The views expressed in this work are solely those of the author and do not necessarily reflect the views of the publisher, and the publisher hereby disclaims any responsibility for them.

Any people depicted in stock imagery provided by Getty Images are models, and such images are being used for illustrative purposes only. Certain stock imagery © Getty Images.

Cover Illustration by Nick DePasquale

Scripture taken from the King James Version of the Bible.

Scripture taken from the New King James Version® Copyright © 1982 by Thomas Nelson. Used by permission. All rights reserved.

ISBN: 978-1-6642-4882-3 (sc)
ISBN: 978-1-6642-4881-6 (hc)
ISBN: 978-1-6642-4883-0 (e)

Library of Congress Control Number: 2021922207

Print information available on the last page.

WestBow Press rev. date: 11/20/2021

Isaiah 41:10
Fear not, for I am with you;
Be not dismayed, for I am your God.
I will strengthen you,
Yes, I will help you,
I will uphold you with My righteous right hand.'

Endorsements

❖ Wow! Having lost my own wife only a month before reading this book, I give it my highest recommendation. Jean Ann is raw and transparent and drew me in from the first sentence. It was completely relatable and comforted me knowing I was not alone in my grief. This book is anointed and will benefit those suffering loss. I cried through much of it and every tear shed brought relief and healing.

Dr. Tim Henderson
Lead Pastor Jonathan Creek Christian Church, Sullivan, IL
Public Speaker, Author, Broadcast Personality

❖ Jean Ann's personal story and suggestions for healing has been immensely helpful and necessary for me to begin and continue my healing process after suddenly losing my husband. My pain is being eased after reading her timely book.

Roben Levine

Foreword

If I didn't know these people personally, I would think that the contents of this book are an excellent narrative; a well-written novel of some sort, but it's a true account of two people's lives and how they overcame their struggles.

Indeed, there is power in the Blood of Jesus. The testimony and memories shared throughout the pages of this book are evidence of lives lived prior to being followers of Christ, lives that existed in crisis, and what can happen when a man and woman turn their imperfect lives over to a powerful God who is more than capable to turn their lives around.

Are their lives perfect? Keep reading. Their story, struggles, the love shared, the ministry, the tragedy, and their living beyond being shattered, pulls you into their world, displaying their humanity and showcasing the miracle-working power of God.

Is it possible? "With God, all things are possible."

I have had the pleasure of knowing Jean Ann and Nick DiBenedetto for many years. However, I never knew before reading this book all that they've been through and how far our Lord Jesus Christ has brought them.

A life determined to strive and live for Christ can push through the most profound struggles, anguishes of mental and emotional turmoil. What God has done in their lives, God can do for you. Like the DiBenedetto's, you too can find the mender of broken hearts.

I pray these pages are a blessing to you, as they have been to me.

Well done, my dear friend Nick DiBenedetto. One day, "When we all get to heaven What a day of rejoicing that will be When we all see Jesus, We'll sing and shout the victory. (Songwriters: Bill Wolaver / E.e. Hewitt / E.d. Wilson)

Rev. Dr. Dan Correa
Lead Pastor Middletown, NJ Assembly of God,
Middletown, NJ Asamblea de Dios
Iglesia Vida Abundante Asamblea de Dios
Police Chaplain
Author-Crazy Faith

I have had the opportunity to know Jean Ann DiBenedetto for quite a few years now. I have known her as an evangelist, speaker, worshiper, minister, encourager and a full-fledged, sold out, lover of the Lord. I have had the opportunity to know, first hand, her love for her family as well. Jean Ann is a mother, a Nonna, a sister, a daughter and friend. Perhaps the greatest way that I have had the blessing to witness Jean Ann, was as a wife. To see Jean Ann, was to see Nick. Together they shared one of the most beautiful love stories I've been blessed to witness. They were a joy to watch, as I'm a bit of a people watcher, and a true inspiration to many couples walking through the fire of trials and tribulations in marriage.

The last word that I would ever associate with Jean Ann is *shattered* and yet, I understand perfectly. The reason I understand is that I too have been shattered by the loss of a spouse during this COVID-19 pandemic and shattered is more than an adequate word to describe the loss, depression, fear, etc., that is encountered at losing your partner, your best friend and the earthly love of your life.

In this beautiful homage to Nick, Jean Ann has shown us how she dealt with his illness and ultimately his graduation to worship God face to face. The way she has found strength and comfort is by seeking God, our comforter and our healer. The One who will make all things new in His time and the One who will help Jean Ann, myself and others who have lost and are feeling lost, to find a new, deeper identity in Him.

As you read through the pages of this book, I pray that you'll see Jean Ann and her heart and that you see that although Nick was her everything, ultimately God is everything to Jean Ann. I recall being at a women's retreat one time and being presented with a picture of a broken vessel that was glued back together and was imperfect. In those imperfections is where God's light shines through. You, Jean Ann and I are those broken vessels and God **will** shine his light through the brokenness. Cling to Him, Jehovah Rapha, and never let go.

Yvette Mendez

Dedication

I dedicate this book to my husband of forty-five years and nine months. He was the man I was with for almost forty-eight years. To the man who made me a wife, mother and a woman. He loved me the best way he knew – only too bad I realized it when it was too late. He dealt with an inner turmoil that no one could understand including me. Combine that with pain of failure, regret and loss, and you have a man who no one knew but inwardly cried out to be loved.

God blessed me with a man who loved me no matter what. He took my faults, weight gain, imperfections and intense stubbornness and loved me with a fire in his soul that burned until the day we parted. He was a father who would die for his boys and one who worked sometimes three jobs so as to give his sons the latest and the best. A grandpa, who now had lost a lot of patience due to the constant pain he was in, yet would pray for his grandchildren and cry when we spoke of them because of the love in his heart for each one. He was SO PROUD of his family!

I dedicate this book to the man who daily spoke these words to me; "I love you Jean Ann, you are a classy woman." Not a time went by after preaching did he not utter … "I am so proud of you." I dedicate this book to a man I wish was alive here on earth to see it as he deserved it a long time ago.

He called me babe and I often told him that he was my #2 as Jesus was #1. Never will that change as he will always be #2 in my heart. I always loved him, love him still and will always love him. I will forever love you Nicky.

December 29, 2020
The Beginning of the End

The phone rang …

My husband: "Hello."

Voice on the other end: "Mr. DiBenedetto, I'm sorry to have to tell you, but you tested positive for Covid."

My husband: "What about the antibiotic I was supposed to pick up at the pharmacy?"

Voice on the other end: "Don't worry about it, just quarantine yourself in a separate bedroom and use a separate bathroom. I'm so sorry to be a bearer of bad news."

My husband: "Ok."

Voice on the other end: "I'm so sorry Mr. DiBenedetto."

My husband: "Ok, (pause) bye."

My immediate response: "This is because I have told you to shower and change your clothes when you come home, but you didn't take me seriously!" (I was not nice to him).

Side note: my husband was diagnosed with Lymphoma (cancer in lymph nodes) months prior and had been going for his treatment. When I yelled at him, it was because I did not feel the treatment center was very sanitary due to hundreds going in and out daily. Each day he visited the center I requested that he shower and change clothes as soon as he came home, but he would rebel.

My response continued: "I think you need to find a place to quarantine. Our grandchildren live here, what about them?"

Without hesitation he packed a bag and left to stay at a nearby motel for three days. I would bring him food and Gatorade in my trunk and would back up to the motel door for him to take it out without us having any contact. It was horrible and I HATED knowing he was in that place ... I HATED IT!

After three days I told him to come home as the family had gone to the Midwest. He did and stayed in the bedroom burning with fever. I placed a little table outside the bedroom door (so he didn't have to bend down) where I would leave food, Gatorade and water. We would talk on the phone and facetime during the day. His fever was not going away and he would not eat a single thing. I began to get sharp with him to force him to eat, but to no avail. We'd pray together each time the fever would spike. We prayed first thing in the morning in faith for a good day however it did not seem to be getting better. My sister would bring Tylenol, something to stop the diarrhea, Pedialyte and protein bars and shakes. She would drop them off outside our kitchen door and leave as I too was now in quarantine. The whole thing makes me cry as it was a horrible experience.

After a few days I realized it was time to share it with our children. Immediately our son Nick informed me that he and his family would get into the car and come to take care of Daddy. I rejected the idea, but he was adamant about it. His response was, "keep him alive until we get there and I will stay in the room and take care of him." Again I rejected that because I did not want him or his family getting the virus. He sharply responded, "I will stay in the room with him, make sure he eats and keep him company to lift his spirits." (I am crying as I can hear those words ... oh my heart). Even though my concern for my son was made clear, he was not having it and within hours they were on their way. Upon hearing this, my husband was the happiest I have seen him in a long time. He could not wait to see his son!

He wanted a haircut before seeing his family so I bundled up, set up and covered a chair and onto the deck we went.

One Picture Says A Thousand Words

This picture says it all. My daughter-in-law Andrea (no it's not her birthday or special occasion) I just want to say how much I love her! As soon as they heard that my husband was not doing well, they jumped in their car and drove from the Midwest straight through (20 hours). Andrea stepped up to the occasion and took over as my husband's private nurse. In addition, she would not let me do a thing. She washed laundry, served food, went shopping and bossed us all around.

That didn't stop once things changed. She decided when I could not do it, she planned and organized, booked a van and stocked it with goodies so our family could stay together during a tender time in our lives. She worked overtime on paper work and making sure I got things done without hesitation. Her last words every night were, "anything else?" As exhausted as she was, her last words were always, "What needs to be done?" She took the load off of me in every way. She made sure things got done that I could never do alone. I told my son that he married a gem and I want to thank her with all my heart. My husband would ask day after day; "How's my daughter?" Well, she proved to be just that. God bless this young lady and give her the desires of her heart. My daughter-in-law, Andrea Joy DiBenedetto … she brings just that … Joy! I love her with all my heart and want to honor her. Thank you, Andrea, for always going the second mile and beyond.

The Raging Fire

I'm sure there will be a day when the hurt will not be as profound, but right now it's sharper than a sword with edges. Sometimes the crying is one big yell, exhaling with a huge gust of PAIN! Just to see his face! Just to touch his face again! *Deep love ... **real love** ... is not a feeling.* It's when a commitment is made before God, for better or for worse, and no matter what, with God's help you look past the faults, read between the lines and give one hundred percent to that one you are committed to.

August 8, 1973

Honorable Discharge from the United States Army

Nicholas D. DiBenedetto Jr.
Spec. 4 United States Army

Nicholas D. DiBenedetto Jr. was picked up by his parents at the airport. What should have been a time of elation was turned into a lifelong nightmare. While Nick Sr. was driving the car, an excited mother was seated in the passenger seat (her son was finally home after serving two long years in Germany during the Vietnam War). Nicholas (who later would be my husband) slid to the floor in the back seat of that car, where he laid until arriving home.

"No Nick the light fixture is not melting," exclaimed his mother the following morning. "I know it's not, but I see it melting," cried her extremely tormented son. All through the night he was up seeing things melt and observing the movements of his hands. He watched each second as he would turn the light switch on or pick up a cigarette. He was tormented in ways no one knew how to deal with, so off they went to the nearest Veteran's Hospital where their loving son unexpectedly was admitted for a stay.

This stay lasted for five months. During his time there he spent much time in solitary confinement (in a padded room) as no one knew exactly what to do with him. He was diagnosed with schizophrenia (multiple personalities). Medication was the answer and consistent visits with a psychiatrist.

He was often visited by an evil presence that was sucking him into the bed. Deeper and deeper he would go until he realized that if he gave in he would be in hell, so each time he shouted out, "JESUS!" The evil presence would dissipate until it had a mind to return. After five months of VA membership, he was notified that they were scheduling him to be admitted to a long-term facility where he would live. Knowing this, he faked his way out. He said he would daily see people walk the halls and scream out vulgarities or take a running start from the end of the hall and sprint to the opposite end and fling themselves into the barred window. Experiencing this nightmare day after day, he was terrified to be placed in a long-term facility, so he faked his way out.

Upon returning home little had changed. He would watch his steps as he walked and intently take note as the refrigerator door would swing each time it opened. He found himself in a black hole that he did not know how to get out of. After returning visits to the hospital, moving into his own apartment and an unsuccessful attempt at suicide he was on the weekly payroll at the psychiatrist's office.

One year later:

While sitting at the kitchen table of the boy I was about to break up with, in walked Nick DiBenedetto. Long hair flowed down his back, he had a full beard that reached to his chest and was missing front teeth, which I later found out were knocked out for the SECOND time in a fight. He was repulsive to say the least and was not my cup of tea so to speak. He asked me out on a date for the following night and I told him I'd have to think about it. After my ex-boyfriend's two sisters convinced me, I replied with a yes. "Don't get dressed too good, we're only going to the park," he said. WHAT WAS I THINKING??????

After telling my sister that I was not going to show up, she made me feel guilty because I lied to him, so I showed up. He had a light blue car with one door as the other was smashed in. This was the beginning of what would be close to forty-eight years together. He held my hand as we stood on the bridge talking and the rest is history.

Knowing the relationship had become serious I agreed to accompany him to his weekly sessions with the psychiatrist. Week after week I listened as the doctor blamed one person after another for Nick's issues. First it was his parents and family, but when I was now the cause of his problems (which he had long before we ever met) I decided to end my visits. However, before marriage I did consult with the doctor in regards to the future. His diagnosis was multiple personalities coupled with depression and he would be on medication for the rest of his life.

After being involved in a relationship for more than a year, the feelings surpassed the diagnosis, so we moved forward into marriage. Many nights were spent trying to console him and calm his emotions, but I was of little help. He would constantly tell me how he fell in love with my mind and such wisdom I had, yet I had no answers to bring his inner turmoil to an end. There were red flags before the wedding, but I was in deep. No one in my family had agreed with our marriage, but there was something I saw deep inside this man that made me melt.

Not long after the wedding the nightmare got worse. I was just a teen and he was almost eight years my senior. It was his way or no way for a very long time. I saw emotions turn within a heartbeat and was oblivious to the solution. There was something inside this man that was wonderful yet it was often times like living with Dr. Jekyll and Mr. Hyde.

It wasn't until after we were sharing coffee at our kitchen table and he jumped up, flung coffee at me, shouted a few choice words and left our apartment that he realized there was a problem. When returning home he was a bit angry at me for not being receptive to his affection, at which time the person who was there and had witnessed the incident with the coffee explained to him what he had done. He was stunned and had no recollection of what he had said or done. I lived with this for the first part of our marriage, with our first son and our second was on his way.

We May Have Fooled The People, But We Never Fooled God

One year after our marriage, I had developed a dependency to alcohol that resulted in an ulcer. It was at that time through a series of events that we were introduced to Jesus as our Lord and Savior. It was a very difficult time and our lives became more tumultuous with every moment. We went to church for six years one way, but returned home another. Our relationship with Jesus was not there, we had been attending a very good Bible believing and preaching church with an amazing pastor, but we had not been willing to surrender. We held onto our lifestyle … smoking, drinking and I just knew that he had been unfaithful. Our marriage was fist fights and struggle yet we were attending church with our phony smiles and hypocritical lifestyle. *We may have fooled the people but we never fooled God.* Our pastor dealt with a lot yet never gave up on us.

Pastor and Sister Schaefer who led us to Jesus and gave us our roots

It was a church where we were blessed to sit under a pastor that believed in the WHOLE truth of God's Word. It wasn't just a Bible … it was God's Word. Our pastor believed that if God delivered people from demons in Bible days He could deliver people today. Thank you Pastor Schaefer. Knowing that, he had my husband at the altar where he prayed over him with such authority and love. Service after service hands were being laid upon my husband and I in prayer until one Sunday morning my husband began to cough so much that he could not catch his breath. He ran out of the church and vomited on the ground and cried out to Jesus. Some may not believe this and think it is nonsense, but I was there and can attest to the fact that a new beginning had begun.

I had experienced the spiritual darkness in our home on numerous occasions and the battle was real. You see, it's not enough to just attend church or ask Jesus to be our Savior. We've got to be willing to repent (turn away from our sinful lifestyle) and surrender to Jesus and allow Him to be our LORD as well as our Savior.

A lot of people attend church and want to know why nothing changes or why they are so downcast or without hope and racked with fear and unbelief in times of trial. It's because church never saved

anybody — Jesus saves people! It is imperative that we attend a good Bible believing, Bible preaching church and surround ourselves with the family of God. This is mandatory in order for us to have a victorious and vibrant life. However, that is not enough. We all must be willing to see our disobedient, sinful lifestyle for what it is, repent and ask God to forgive us. Believe that Jesus died on the cross for us and took our place for our sins. Ask for His forgiveness, invite Him into our hearts and lives and surrender our will to His with a determination to live pleasing to His Word. This is for all of us.

Well in time we were both ready to surrender … to yield our will to the will of our Heavenly Father. Jesus became Lord of our lives, our family and our home. The call came upon my husband as the burden for those without Jesus caused him much sorrow. He cried often over those who were deceived in religion without the knowledge of salvation in Jesus. He wept and knew that God had called him to as he put it: "go fishing." His first message was entitled "Nobody's Fishing." He was called to fish for souls as he believed God called him to be a fisher of men.

The Turmoil Rages

It was past midnight, standing against the microwave in my mother's kitchen, that he opened up and wept for hours. Junk was pouring out as he unloaded years of guilt and shame. He was as transparent as glass in a store window as story after story, event after event was unraveling from years past. He poured out his heart like I've never seen nor heard before. He was certain that he was too bad for God's forgiveness. He cried to the point of being almost unrecognizable. He began to reveal the evil he had been hiding since childhood. While growing up in the projects he had been part of a gang and watched out for the police. He saw and heard things that no person should ever witness. I know what was revealed to me, but it will never to be disclosed, as it's not fit for anyone to hear. I gave him my word and it has never slipped through my lips as it was a past lifestyle of which he didn't know any better and the Blood of Jesus had cleansed him from it all. Jesus took those (his and mine) sins at the cross!

He threw himself onto my mother's kitchen table and wept until sun up. I laid my body across his and held him in my arms rebuking the enemy of his soul and praying until breakthrough came. He cried for weeks proclaiming his adoration and love for Jesus.

Following the call we pursued ministry for our Lord as he was called to be an Evangelist. We began with singing ... he had a voice like no one I ever heard, it was smooth and put you right into whatever song he sang. His voice was amazing! We traveled for twenty-one years as a family ministering all across the United States.

Such times of great anointing yet moments of melancholy came. Sorrow and depression was taking over. Days filled with grouchiness and anger would overtake our lives. Nicky would sleep for hours in a day, not wanting to speak with anyone or even practice our harmony. He rebelled and loved all at the same time. He loved his family yet at times acted the complete opposite. He was becoming more and more unhappy and the struggle became more evident.

The initial diagnosis years earlier were upon us! The inability to make normal decisions or have a decent conversation without arousing an argument became more frequent. Our boys were pulling away. I wanted to run but was committed. I knew it was wrong to leave and deep down inside I loved him. He was the father of my three boys! He was so good on the inside … what was going on? Was the previously diagnosed mental illness coming to the surface?

To make a phone call was a chore, or deciding. Actions and reactions at times like a child. The immaturity was frustrating because more was expected from an adult but was not there. He was withdrawing into a world of his own at times resulting in poor choices. What was I to do? I did not know what to do! We argued and fought, not like before we knew the Lord. Fistfights were no longer but arguing was overtaking our lives and we were a hurting family. We didn't want to be that way but we were a hurting family ministering to hurting families. We were steeped into ministry and couldn't turn back. People were turning their hearts to Jesus, families were being reunited, lives were being transformed. Prisons were experiencing the Presence of God as we would come in with five-part harmony and usher in a Presence that melted the hardest heart. The Lord was moving in such a mighty way! Teen Challenges (men & women's homes) across America were being affected by the anointing upon Go Ye Ministries, the DiBenedetto Family. What were we to do? Who were we to talk to? God was moving in spite of us, but we as a family were hurting and needed help. No one was there. We were the ministers who were supposed to have all the answers so why should we need help?

We were hurting and I reached out for help, but no one had an answer. Nicky was filled with such love, yet the turmoil was raging. This went on for years and for years I opened up to my colleagues … the ones who were supposed to know that same Jesus we knew. Not one single person reached out to my husband, not one.

On three separate occasions I left the man I loved. Nothing could stop me from loving my husband … nothing. He was my husband and I loved him like crazy because I saw a side of him that no one else saw. He knew me like no one else knew me. He was my husband, friend, lover, companion and ministry partner. Nicholas DiBenedetto was a great man! I loved a great man! He was my husband

and I wanted to stand by him no matter what but we needed help. I am so very sorry to admit this but the church was of no help. I reached out to friends, numerous people we loved and knew loved us, but one single person responded, our amazing friend Carol. Years of hurting and not wanting to hold the bag alone yet one single person, Carol … not one other reached out to help.

The Elephant in the Room

Something that was bigger than life reared its ugly head on a daily basis, but it never revealed its identity. My husband, as kind and gentle of a man that he was, oftentimes was wrapped within this thing ... this thing that robbed him of his identity. This thing was huge and it claimed his joy, peace and freedom of mind. Nicky was a good man and loved me and his family and would give his life for any one of us. He loved his family! I'm telling you – he was a great man! Unfortunately this thing that wrapped him up was killing all of us. Our sons eventually went onto lives of their own, but I was still living with this thing. I loved him and we loved each other but this thing got in the way constantly.

We prayed and fasted and cried out to God. We fought and made up and assured each other of our affection, loyalty and love but it was so hard. We finally had an agreement that there would be times I would have to go away for a week or so for a breather. He knew why and was ok with this agreement. I attended many ministers' functions alone as he was not in the frame of mind to join. I always wished he had attended because he loved being together with fellow servants, but every time we left saddened by the politics and hypocrisy of the leaders. Pastors oftentimes shy away from the evangelists to avoid being asked to hold a service in their church. What they do not know is that we all need each other and that being an evangelist is especially difficult because of the sacrifice of not being in our home church weekly and it takes a toll.

I've come to a place of realization that true believers, the "family" of God have the attributes of my Heavenly Father. If love and compassion is missing … it's missing. Truth be told, the reason no one responded to my plea for help with my husband is because they did not know what to do. All good people who love the Lord, but lacking the sacrifice of the time it takes to be alone with the Lord, until He speaks direction for the next step is taboo. Too much saying instead of praying is obvious. *We as a church need to get alone with God and hear His voice or we will be powerless in all situations.* Not many want to be a friend to the one suffering depression. Not because people are bad but because people are empty. Knowing what to do or say is not there and it takes time to take time. When we finally found a pastor who was willing to speak with us he fell asleep on us in our meeting. And this is why we have taught our children to never look up to a man because if that man falls you will fall with him. *Respect those in authority over you but never look up to anyone but Jesus.* He will never fall and neither will you.

So what was the elephant in the room? What my husband was dealing with was not his alone, it was affecting everyone around him. It made for a very unpleasant atmosphere and many just thought it was easier to avoid the elephant instead of addressing it. How do you address an elephant? The Bible says that LOVE covers a multitude of sin. *When my feelings become more important than what others are going through, there's a plank in my eye.* So before I am to be concerned with the toothpick in my brother's eye it would be a better idea to address the plank in my own.

No one's aspirations are to be nasty and unliked by all, if that's the case then there's a problem. What is the problem? There's an elephant in the room! It's big and unavoidable so let's just ignore it right? I am so sorry to say this but *many who claim to be part of the family of God need to denounce the Spirit of Religion and take on the Spirit of God.* It's the Love of God that changes hearts. You cannot win a soul until you win a friend. **We are not called to accept someone's sin – we are called to love them out of it.**

Actions were reactions to the torment my husband lived with. Yes you can call it a demon and rightly so, but it was what it was. Revisiting back to my mother's kitchen - he was confessing many things. Things that he could not get out of his heart and pictures that tormented his mind were robbing him of the very thing that Jesus shed His blood for on the cross at Calvary ... FORGIVENESS! Although he could pray for many and many times he did. Although he had a burden for the hurting and those rejected, he too was hurting and felt rejected. Early in his life, before surrendering his heart and life to Jesus, he had made many poor choices which haunted him forever. He believed he was unworthy, did too much bad to make it right. True, *you can never make a wrong a right,* but JESUS FORGIVES ... AND WE CAN BE BORN AGAIN!

Unfortunately Nicky in many ways raised himself. He would oftentimes collect his father at the bar and staggered home to his mother. He stood by his mother and nothing was going to hurt her. He often took the beatings from a drunk father to avoid her from getting hurt. He had an older brother dealing with life controlling issues himself and my husband would take the punishment for him because he loved his mother, yet his mother favored his brother and it would hurt her to see him get beat up, so my husband often took the strap (with the buckle shaped in an N for Nick). As I was told his mother would blame the empty bottles of alcohol on my husband when they were hers or her son's (not Nick) and he would take the brunt of it. When his brother came home late and too high to walk, my husband would hide his brother under the bed so dad (who was often intoxicated) did not see him. He started working at nine years old at an Italian Grocery Store (Celentano's by name ... yes, the famous ravioli company) learning how to make mozzarella just to bring his money home to give to his mother, but not until years later realizing that he did all he can to love his mother yet it was very obvious that she had a favorite and Nicky was not it. He watched out for her and expressed to me many times how he had to pour her into bed intoxicated in the daytime so she could be ok when his father came home, yet his love for her was so great that he never thought anything was wrong with that. He was taught to honor her and honor her he did until the day she passed.

Not long after we were married his father was diagnosed with cancer. My husband sat by his side in the hospital without leaving. The beatings didn't matter, the cursing, etc. didn't matter. He told me; "he is my father." He walked with him, prayed with him, made all medical decisions and was with him until his last breath.

The dreaded disease of emphysema encamped within his mother's lungs … she was very ill. My husband was loyal to his mother. His sister had passed a few years before his mom, leaving her alone, and my husband took on all financial obligations. Once a month I would go food shopping and stock her pantry … she wanted for nothing. I would insist on trying to get her senior assistance but he insisted that she was his mother and he was going to take care of her even if it was our own money. The day my mother-in-law passed away in the hospital my husband was informed that she had disowned him. He was not left in the will and she did not want him to bury her. I have a copy of the will that states that she bequeaths nothing to her son Nicholas due to past experiences. We were then told that we owed her money that was not paid. Even after she was gone there was a lie about my husband.

I watched a man's face turn burgundy and become like a brick. He sat on the sofa and stared for hours. The pain gripped every part of him … he could not speak. He stared into space like a zombie yet when it was all over and he until the day he too went home to be with Jesus never found out if she was cremated or buried and he still would not say a negative word about her. He cried to me many, many times over it … MANY times. However, he always followed up by expressing his love for her and how he was not sorry that he stood up for her, stood by her side and took upon himself all her needs. He would say; "she was my mother." As angry at him as I would get at times, I am so very proud of him as a man who stood his ground no matter what and knew how to honor his parents.

My husband was such a good man with more love and compassion in his heart than most. He loved me and I knew it, he loved his boys and would run when they called, his grandchildren held a special place of pride and adoration in his heart. He would give his life in a second for anyone in his family. Although we often didn't understand his actions he loved us all. I am so very sorry to admit that I did not always treat him with understanding. It was harder than I can explain but one thing never changed and that was the deep love I always had for him. He was the only man I have ever given my all to and loved more than my own life.

No matter how good he was he could not forgive himself. All he saw was what he had done wrong, he knew forgiveness was for all, but to accept it for himself seemed to be an impossibility. It wasn't tangible; it wasn't a reality to him. Although he wanted it to be a reality he had found it impossible to forgive himself. Maybe it was the way he was treated by those professing to know what love was ... I don't know. Maybe it was because Satan knew the call upon his life and how mighty of a man my husband was, so he did all he could to subdue it ... I don't know. Maybe it was because his entire life was one of giving and loving, but it never seemed to be enough for him to get in return. Not from his parents or even his ex-girlfriend, who was unfaithful at home while he was away giving his life for our country. To him no one was loyal or he wasn't good enough for anyone to love.

One thing I do know and it's that *those of us who are in the family of God need to learn how to love like our Heavenly Father does* (myself included). Our Heavenly Father would not reject us, so why should we reject one of His children? He always has time for us. Why is it that we become so preoccupied with talking about reaching those in need instead of helping those in need?

Many are dealing with an elephant in the room. May it be that all don't live up to our expectations? Whatever it may be, it may make us uncomfortable. After reading this my desire is that it would convict our hearts enough to bring our flesh under submission to

God and ask for His forgiveness and His love. Let the love of Jesus ooze out of each of us. How many could we help?

My husband loved Jesus with all his heart. He was a man on a mission; a mission to help people. It hurt his heart to see someone on the wrong path and I am hearing stories now of lives that have been touched and turned around because of the Love of Jesus shared by him. He knew what a Pentecostal handshake (money in the hand) was, even if he didn't have it to give. He could not see anyone going without or hurting. Many times he would come home from work and share with me the need to pray for someone and we did. He cared like Jesus cared. I will forever be proud and grateful for the stories I am hearing about his sacrificial love and concern for others.

I believe his compassion was birthed out of the reality of living in pain himself. I don't believe he wanted anyone to go through the mental and emotional torment he himself had to endure. *Mental illness is huge but the Love and Forgiveness of God is even greater.* Oh, how I wish he would have forgiven himself.

So many engulfed in building their own ministry or kingdom here on earth are unlike the man I married, he was engulfed in building the kingdom. Nicky, if you could only see how the Lord used you.

The Pain Continues ...
He Had to Work

Ten to twelve years into marriage he began to experience pain in one of his knees. This was due to the bending many times a day to set a car on a lift (he was an auto mechanic) and he just ignored it ... he had to work. As time went on it became both knees. It went from pain to agony but ... he had to work. Before long his legs were becoming bowed, which we later realized was caused by trying to work with the pain, so it knocked his gate off. He learned how to make it day after day with a minor adjustment in his walk. Instead of taking care of his knees with rest ... he had to work. Due to the unfair adjustment in his walking he now began to feel it in his hip. Instead of taking care of the issues at hand ... he had to work.

In addition to the pain of two knees and a hip, we were now noticing bumps popping up on his wrists and hands, his finger began to bend a bit. His neck was in pain, before long it was his arms, wrists, back ... all the way to his feet. The pain was all the time so he was quickly diagnosed with arthritis attacking his spine. Arthritis ran rampant throughout his entire body causing pain everywhere. Couple the pain of arthritis with two knees that were now bone on bone and a hip bone on bone in addition to mental illness and you have a man that is in constant torment. However, torment or not ... he had to work.

Although he was past retirement age bills had to be paid. He was concerned that there would not be enough coming in through the ministry and he did not want me to be concerned. Little did he know that my faith has always been in my Heavenly Father and knew that He was my provider and miracle worker if need be, but ... he had to work.

For years he faced physical pain and mental torment living on Tylenol or Ibuprofen, but he would not take a thing for the emotional pain. I believe he was always on edge with too much medication due to the fact that he was a former drug user. Before coming to Christ he took everything with the exception of heroin as he wouldn't put a needle in his arm. His drug of choice was smoking pot or snorting cocaine and before our marriage the doctor had him on so much valium that he could not function normally without it. Knowing his former habits, I believe there was always that little fear of becoming dependent once again. Most nights were now spent on the same recliner he was also on for many hours in a day. He would dangle his feet to relieve the pressure on his back and sit in a straight up position to try and alleviate the pain. Night after night was the ritual of moaning and shouting out in pain. Before the crack of dawn he was up and ready to face another day and walked down the stairs one step at a time. The pain was intense and became numb to all medication. It was hard for him to believe that God would heal his body as he still dealt with the elephant in the room of the why. Why would God heal me? What have I done to deserve His healing and forgiveness?

That pain overtook his life ... but he had to work. As time went by, his place of employment noticed that he could no longer climb the stairs, so they moved him to a sitting position. That was a blow that kicked his ego in the pants. He cried as we sat and talked, he felt like he was failing in every area of life and fell deeper into the pit of despair. Through it all he always had a song within him. I would oftentimes catch him listening to a song by Clint Brown entitled "Waiting on You". It was directed to the Lord as his heart would cry out to his Heavenly Father.

After being relocated to line work, little did his employer know that it was a physical nightmare for my husband. Arthritis had taken over his hands so although he was sitting, having to work consistently with his hands was leaving him in AGONY! He was in pain twenty-four hours a day from his head to his feet, but … he had to work. He would wrap his arms around me and tell me how much he loved me and I would respond with a heartless, "show me you love me, don't tell me." How WRONG I WAS!!! He WAS showing me! He had to work! My husband was not physically well for most of our married life and not mentally well for its entirety. He was the most misunderstood man around beginning with me.

I knew his pain and saw his diligence through it all but the repercussions of it made for a very difficult go of it. Though the love that I had for him was deep, it was EXTREMELY difficult for me to go day to day with expecting more instead of understanding that he was giving his all. I am so sorry! Pain, depression and self-condemnation made for a tormented man and oftentimes all I saw was the results of it.

We prayed often together, we talked, went to church and discussed solutions but nothing panned out. He was facing a dead-end wall daily and it was taxing upon my being to say the least. Over and over again I would reach out to a fellow minister for help but to no avail. Not one single person took the time to talk to this man who loved Jesus with all his heart but misunderstood and was swept under a rug. Not by me! He was not going to be swept under a rug by me!

I cried out to my God and drew my strength from Him and waited. I waited to hear His Voice thousands of times and it was always the same, "Love him." Even when I could not bear it any longer and took off, there was no peace within as I heard my God's Voice. "You will not divorce this man", I tried … I tried to love him with everything inside of me. No matter how hard it was I tried to love him and understand the pain he was living with but my patience wore thin and it was just plain hard. Everyone had gone and it was just he and I. What appeared to be abuse to me was just his frustration of living in a manner that was not who he really was inside. He was a good man!

Daily facing his pain and trials yet … he had to work. Knowing it was going to be a rough day depending upon the weather … he had to work. Even the many times I tried to talk some sense into him and have important conversations regarding our future or what would happen if one of us should pass. He could not mentally deal with it, yet … he had to work.

I believe work was his way to say to me, "Jean Ann, don't worry about anything, I love you." Limited as he may have been in some areas, his love for me was not and I knew it. I was his wife and he loved me and sang to me until days before going home to glory. Many would have curled up and died but my husband fought through it all on a daily basis proving to our family the man that he was and in our hearts forever will be.

Hades in the Hospital

Before our son and his family arrived from the Midwest my husband's health was already failing. He could not tolerate food of any sort, I would cook his favorite foods but into the garbage it would go. His body was getting too weak to fight the infection (Covid 19). I would not let him rest as I tried to keep him on the phone constantly fighting with him to take in nutrition so he could build his strength. We laughed as I overheard him through the ceiling call me the wicked witch of the west as we ended our conversation. I playfully yelled up, "I HEARD THAT!" We laughed as I then answered the phone with, "the wicked witch of the west here." We were trying to make light of a very heavy time.

Nicky was getting weaker and I noticed his labored breathing on the phone. I prayed for him consistently, quoted scriptures, sang songs of worship and deliberately let him know how much I loved him. I forced him to go outside on our deck to take in a few deep breaths of fresh air. Bundled in clothes, his infamous black leather jacket, hat, mask and gloves he crept down the stairs one step at a time while gasping for air. I watched as he tried to walk in the sunshine but had to hold onto the railing as he was too weak to stand. Before the day was up the oximeter was reading alarmingly low. He was running a fever and breathing heavy. I was all alone watching the fear in his eyes as he looked at me like a scared little boy. My heart was aching! I did NOT want to put him in the hospital! If he would only eat I thought he would build some strength to fight.

911 had to be called and the ambulance drove off to the nearest hospital. I wanted to die! The PAIN watching him - the once strong, very strong man who could pick up the back end of a car with no problem - was now barely able to walk to the door. MY HEART WAS ACHING!!!! I WAS SO CONCERNED ABOUT HIM!!! I cried out to God as my heart sunk watching the flashing lights rolling down our driveway. Watching until the lights were no more I went inside the house only to weep before God in PAIN! I DID NOT WANT TO SEE HIIM GO THROUGH THIS!!! WHAT COULD I DO TO HELP HIM???? OH HOW I LOVED HIM!!!! I CRIED OUT TO GOD!!!!! All alone in that house the realization of the severity of his illness gripped my heart! OH HOW I LOVE HIM!!! GOD, PLEASE HEAL HIS BODY ... PLEASE!!!!! I cried out to God from places in my heart I have never been.

Kicking into gear I began to wash and sanitize the room that he had been in. I was doing everything I could to make our home safe but not without pain. The PAIN of knowing he was going to a place where they would not look after him like I would was KILLING me!

He was in the hospital, but knowing his son was coming, he insisted on coming home. Our granddaughter, Nina, was flying in to see grandpa and he was not having it, he was coming home no matter what anyone said because he wanted to see his granddaughter. The nurse explained the severity of his sickness on the phone to me but he was not having it! He was coming home to see his Nina before she had to return!

Our son, Nicky, went to pick him up at the hospital. My heart was rejoicing because I could not wait to see him yet I was totally confused as to why the hospital ordered oxygen to be delivered to our home prior to his discharge. No one prepared me for what I was to see next! Excitedly I ran to the deck and looked down only to see my husband unable to get out of the car without assistance from our son, holding onto his arm for dear life and barely walking at a crawl's pace with oxygen connected to his nostrils. For the first time in my life I swallowed a lump in my throat of pain that felt like a bowling ball. I ran into the house but could not speak. Locking myself in the bathroom I threw my face into a towel and wailed. I wailed until I could no longer. The PAIN of seeing him in that state wrapped around my heart like an iron fist. I could barely breathe without PAIN. I cried and cried with my face in the towel but wanted to wrap my arms around him. I was SO SORRY he was going through this!!! CAN I TAKE THE PAIN AWAY FROM HIM???? I WANT TO TAKE THE PAIN AWAY!!! I DON'T WANT HIM TO GO THROUGH THIS!!!!!! It HURT my heart to see him like this! I cried into that towel!!!

The family stepped up to the plate! He was never alone! Our daughter-in-law, Andrea, took over the job as his private nurse. Our son, Nicky, became his doctor; Anna was the housekeeper and Sal was labeled the slave as he was the runner of all our needs. Nina was designated as my husband's Zoom Coordinator when virtually meeting with the hospital. He was well taken care of.

With arms wrapped around his body and prayers of faith upon my lips I laid by his side in the bed. The heat from his body was not normal and it felt like fire was coming from him. I took his temperature and I was sure it was a mistake … 106?!!! His skin was as red as a beet, his body shivering so I immediately grabbed three wet, ice cold washcloths and wiped him down; his forehead, under his arms and chest while calling upon the Blood of Jesus. No sooner had I put the cloth upon his body the heat was sinking through it. I could not keep the cloths cold long enough to rid him of that fever! We prayed and took authority and stood upon scripture in faith as his life depended upon it!

The Care Team

After his temperature came down, not normal but down enough for me to feel comfortable walking away, I immediately sat down at my computer asking for prayers for my husband. Without specifics I pleaded on Facebook for urgent prayers. I knew that would be the place to have more people praying at the same time! He needed a touch from heaven!

Fever spikes, lack of food and drink consumption and drastic drops in oxygen, it was soon inevitable that he was to be taken to the hospital. With an extremely heavy heart my son Nicky and I drove him to the hospital of our choice. During the entire ride I played the messages on my phone in his ear. Prayers, words of encouragement and scriptures were all played in his ear during that ride. Leaving him in that hospital was the hardest thing I have ever done in my life!

"Ok, you can leave" were the words spoken to me at admitting. I watched as they wheeled him out of sight and my heart ACHED! I did NOT WANT TO LEAVE HIM! However the thought of never seeing him did not enter my mind yet as it was SO HARD to leave him!!!

Two weeks of hades

Nicky and I spoke to each other numerous times a day which was in addition to any updates from the doctor mid-afternoon and the nurse both am and pm. He would constantly tell me how hungry he was and did not like the food. After trying to console him with realizing that hospital food is not the same as home cooked he needed to eat it to keep up his strength. Then he'd complain he was thirsty. After informing me of not having water I urged him to call the nurse. His reply was always the same, "I call the nurse and wait four hours for her to come."

Doctor's and nurse's reports were up and down, it was like a roller coaster. The phone never left my hand! I slept with it in my hand most nights waiting for the early morning call, as I was longing and holding onto my faith that the report would turn positive. Good news ... I was expecting good news. It was up and down but one thing remained consistent, his fever never left. I realized as the moments dragged by how deeply I loved him.

Day after day I begged to see him but I was always refused because he was put onto a Covid floor. Day after day I would ask again and again, "Why is he on a Covid floor if he is not testing positive for Covid?" The response was always the same, "because he has a virus in his system resulting from the Covid Virus and is running a fever." He had developed blood clots in his lungs partnered with pneumonia and a bacterial infection. If he had not been on a Covid floor I would have been able to be with him every day. It was a nightmare! My husband would ask for prayer as he was shaking due to fever spikes. He was drenched in his clothes and not changed.

"Mrs. DiBenedetto, do you want to intubate Mr. DiBenedetto" was the question and I responded with a resounding "NO". "We are trusting God for a miracle" I professed. "There are many people praying for my husband and we are all trusting God as He can do anything," I reiterated.

The Dreaded Call

The following day while our family was visiting our niece's home for Sunday dinner the call came. "Mrs. DiBenedetto, are you alone?" (the life was being sucked out of me) "Is your family with you? Mrs. DiBenedetto, your husband's health has been declining. He is not in good shape as his oxygen level is lowering. I would like to administer morphine." When I asked what that was for it was explained to me as comfort care. It is a method of taking away the discomfort as the patient sleeps off to glory. I told them "NO! Do NOT give him enough morphine to take his life! I do not want him uncomfortable so you can give him enough to comfort him but NOT to take his life."

"I WANT TO SEE HIM," I exclaimed, but the response was that my request would be considered. After speaking with my niece who is a nurse and who was also keeping abreast of it all with the doctor personally, we decided I should go to the hospital immediately.

For Better, For Worse

I sat in silence as my son drove me to the hospital. I wanted to see him! I could not wait to see his face!

I waited in the lobby for what seemed to be eternity. Numerous calls were made to the nurse's station informing them of my arrival and expecting to see my husband. It was always another wait again and again until finally I raised my tone above normal (Italian style) and in no uncertain terms informed them that I was coming up regardless of what they said and that if someone did not come down to get me I was barging through security! "I WANT TO SEE MY HUSBAND NOW!" I exclaimed.

On January 4 at 9:09 p.m. I was accompanied up to his room where I looked at my husband through a window. He was lying on his side with his back to the window, STILL WEARING THE SAME PANTS THAT I DROPPED HIM OFF IN! TEN DAYS LATER AND HE WAS NOT BATHED OR CHANGED! If my heart could speak it would be slobbering out the pain.

After donning myself in protective gear (a hazmat suit) and gloves, I was allowed inside. I quietly stood by his bedside for a few moments until he turned his head and noticed my presence. "JESUS! JESUS! JESUS!" over and over again he shouted the Name of Jesus. "I KNEW YOU WOULD COME, I KNEW YOU WOULD COME, I SAID IF ANYONE COULD GET HERE IT WOULD BE YOU!" "I WAS CALLING YOU! I WAS CALLING YOU! I KNEW YOU WOULD COME! JESUS!!!" He shouted. I threw myself into his arms and held on shouting, "I LOVE YOU! I LOVE YOU NICKY! I LOVE YOU!!!" I moved the oxygen mask to kiss his face. We looked into each other's eyes as we shared our love for one another. I held onto him and did not want to let go! All I could say is I LOVE YOU!

I held onto his arm as I looked into his face and explained ever so gingerly the medical state he was in and how we all were still believing in God for a miracle (I needed to ask what his wishes were regarding intubation). After asking him he agreed in not wanting to be intubated. I tried my best to explain how his lungs took a hit but we were NEVER going to stop believing that our God is a MIRACLE WORKER! He looked into my eyes and whispered, "Am I going to die?" I held him in my arms and repeated, "I love you, I have always loved you and I love you now." I looked into his eyes that were like a little boy's and said, "I LOVE YOU NICKY!!!" I let him know that he is not alone, that the entire family and thousands of people across the world are praying for him. I told him that I was going to walk this with him and never leave him, we were in this together. Over and over we held each other in our arms and expressed how much we loved each other. My heart ACHED!!! *True love is for better or for worse.* It was the worst time of my life but I was going to love him even greater and deeper than I had in the past forty-seven plus years. At that moment he was my world! He was all that mattered to me! I wanted to hold onto him and not let go! It was a love that hurt.

The Mercy of God

He without a breath poured out his heart to me, asking for forgiveness and saying he would never yell at me again. He went on to say that all he did was set his phone on his shoulder and listen to the Bible and with pride he told me that when it was Sunday Morning he let the nurse hear his son Nicky preaching. He said all he did in that hospital was repent. I praised God with him and he repeated, "Babe, I have done nothing but repent and when I get out of here I'm going to preach." He went on to tell me how much he loved his family and his boys were his life. We talked about our boys together and he reassured me not to worry because God was faithful and He would answer my prayers. He mentioned each son by name and spoke specifically about each one and continued on telling me how proud he was of each one of them. He wanted to talk to his grandsons. He asked why he hadn't spoken to Zachary, Caleb and Gideon. He went on to say how he was so blessed with every single one of his grandchildren, how beautiful Nina and Anna were how he loved Salvatore so much and how he enjoyed being with him. He continued on to express his love, pride and adoration for our entire family. With a strategically placed iPad on a stand at his bedside we were able to zoom with everyone! He saw his sons, daughters-in-law, grandchildren, two nieces, his great nephew Antonio and my sister.

His first words to them were how much he loved them and informed them of his love for me and would never yell at me again. It was a wonderful time! It was a desire of both our hearts, to be together as a family. Maybe it wasn't exactly what we would have desired but none the less it was wonderful! The love in that room was so thick you could cut it with a knife. We were zooming from three different states yet it felt like we were sitting around our table sharing a nice Italian meal with crusty bread and topped off with some Italian pastry and an espresso. It was just wonderful! He was SO happy!

Initially I was informed that I would only be allowed fifteen minutes with him but it was thirty minutes later when the nurse alerted me to the rules. After expressions of love all around it was once again Nicky and I. For better or for worse, through sickness and in health, till death do us part … it was us. I kissed his face, stroked my thumb across his lip as I often did, looked him deeply into his eyes, held onto his arm and confessed my love with the realization that I may never see him again. It HURT so bad! HOW CAN I CHANGE THIS? GOD, WE ARE STILL TRUSTING IN YOU FOR A MIRACLE!!! We prayed together, he sang a song to Jesus, we kissed, hugged and exchanged affection. I assured him that I would be back.

With one hand on the door and face towards his ever so frail body I again and again whispered, "I love you Nicky, I love you Nicky" and his response was the same, "I love you Babe." Knowing he had been taken off the covid floor my last words to him were, "I'll be back."

Our last texts to each other

Sunday, January 31, 1:34 PM
Nicholas, I want you to know
that I LOVE YOU!!!!!!!

Sunday, January 31, 2:35 PM
I love you!!!!!!!
Get better!!!! Valentines
Day is coming. Come
home!!!!!

I'm on my way!!!

His Hand Extended

The next four days were brutal. My phone rang. "Mrs. DiBenedetto?" I responded with a yes and was informed, "Mr. DiBenedetto's health is declining and I wanted to know if you wanted me to put the phone to his ear to speak to him." "YES, YES!" I exclaimed. Shaking in my skin I called him by name and knowing the sound of the oxygen was affecting his hearing I spoke loudly. "NICKY, I LOVE YOU NICKY!!! I WANT YOU TO KNOW THAT I WILL ALWAYS LOVE YOU! YOU ARE A GOOD MAN NICKY AND I LOVE YOU WITH ALL MY HEART!" I began to pray still in faith believing for that miracle and again professing my love and the love his entire family has for him. I MADE SURE HE KNEW THAT HIS BOYS LOVED HIM AND THAT HE WAS A GOOD FATHER!

"Hello, Mrs. DiBenedetto are you done?" whispered the nurse on the phone. She continued on to ask me, "Are you a person of faith?" I responded with a yes when she continued on to ask "Are you an evangelist?" "Yes," I responded. She began to let me know that after seeing the last name and hearing me pray she knew who I was and shared how her church loved me each time I ministered there. I asked her if she would do me a favor and she so graciously agreed. I asked her to lay her hands upon my husband's chest and we were going to pray and agree together so she did. We had church! After praying in the Spirit together and agreeing for God to have His way and nothing to stand in His way I thanked her and explained how NOTHING was impossible for God! We shared in agreement, letting her know that I believed she was an angel sent by God and we lovingly parted.

Up and down for the next day. Although my husband was so very short of breath he would sing on the phone songs glorifying Jesus. His last request to me was to pray because he was uncomfortable breathing. I fervently and in faith prayed as he was whispering, "Praise Jesus, Praise Jesus, Praise Jesus." Those were the last words I audibly heard my beautiful husband speak.

That nurse was God's hand extended. The last experience with my husband was prayer and the last words I heard him speak were Praise Jesus. I could not ask for more.

No More

After more forceful measures I was given permission to go into the hospital and visit again. I was so excited and could not wait to see his face! We had just had the worst snowstorm in years and my son was getting ready to dig our car out so that he could drive me to the hospital. Then the phone rang.

"Mrs. DiBenedetto?" "Yes" "I am so sorry to have to say this, but your husband has passed." After a long silence the voice asked, "Are you there?" As I barely responded with a yes she began to share her condolences. I sat in numbness and pain all wrapped up in one. All I could see was his face. I felt a grief that I had never felt before yet a strong stiff peace came over my very being.

Ready to go and dig out the car my son, Vincent, walked down the stairs as I called his name. He walked towards the desk where I was sitting. "Daddy is in no more pain," I said. He stared at me and said "What? You mean ...?" I informed him of the phone call and said, "Daddy is in no more pain, he has no more pain." He walked over to me, wrapped his arms around me and we both wept like babies. Daddy was in no more pain but we were HURTING!!! BADLY we were HURTING!!! "Are you ok?" Vincent lovingly asked me. We held onto each other in tears until it was time to make the phone call and inform his brothers that Daddy had no more pain. Of course it was not easy, Nicky informed that he'd be on the plane as soon as possible and Domenick Raymond wept profusely. Through the hurt each one said the same, "Daddy's in no more pain."

Comfort came! For many years it was comfort that my husband was longing for. It finally came! No more pain, no more sorrow, no more guilt, no more condemnation, no more depression, no more regret, no more, no more, no more. He was finally in the Presence of His Almighty Heavenly Father who I know wrapped His arms around him ... daddy/my husband ... the father of my three sons ... no more pain ... No More.

For the first time in his life I know he was experiencing what real life was and joy that he could only talk about. He experienced the peace that passes all understanding and freedom in his legs to dance. For the first time his heart was experiencing the lightness, as the heaviness was no more. He could squeeze his hands without pain, bend his knees, stand up straight and tall knowing he was somebody ... that he belonged! No more rejection or the loneliness of depression, no more sorrow, no more sickness, no more pain, No More!

My husband did not lose his battle to Covid, he gained his eternal reward. He changed his address and made it home before the rest of us did. We weren't ready to let him go but God in His timing saw that my husband/our boys' dad had suffered long enough. It was time to take him HOME and for that I will forever be grateful. I love my husband, I always have and always will but dealing with mental illness (depression) coupled with physical pain and being misunderstood because of it made for an unhappy man. He deserves to be happy! He is with our family who had gone on before him and I just know that he is holding onto the hand of Jesus and singing of his adoration to him because one thing was for sure - Nicholas DiBenedetto Jr. had a love for Jesus that was not on the surface, it was deep. His love for Jesus was real that at times it caused a disdain for others and even church as he KNEW there was more. He had an experience with the Lord that only he can tell but I know it was one that words could not describe. He loved God and Jesus was his Lord and he was not ashamed of the Gospel of Jesus Christ.

No more, Nicky, no more pain! I'm coming home one day and we will be together forever! I love you!!!

The last text to our boys

Wednesday, February 3, 3:44 AM

Good morning my sons. As you know I can't text from heaven but mommy will share my heart to you. My last conversation with mommy was about you three boys. I told her how proud I was of each of you. How much I love you. I expressed how sorry I was for being the way I was (not very nice or even miserable at times) but while in the hospital I spent most of my time repenting. I'm sorry if I hurt you. I LOVE YOU WITH ALL MY HEART!!! I didn't know how to deal with my demons but my heart was for you ALWAYS!!! I shared with mommy how I could not have asked for more. Although I didn't always show it YOU and mommy are who I lived for. I LOVE YOU!!! I LOVE YOU!!! I LOVE YOU!!!
I want you to know that no one in this world meant more to me than you. I loved watching you grow...my boys...my sons. That's what I told everybody. I told everyone at work about you, showed pictures of my

daughters in law and grandchildren. I am proud of my family...every single one!!!
Nicky, Vincent and Domenick Raymond...my sons. I say that with such pride. You are my world!
Forgive me for not showing it but know that I always said it to mommy. Because of Jesus we will one day be together but until that day, grandma says hi and never...please...never forget how much I LOVE YOU and am SO PROUD OF YOU!!! We will always be together because family is a bond that can never be broken. Please remember that. Feel your chest...I am in your heart and forever you are in mine. I love you three and mommy. I'm proud of my family. And that's what I said to mommy. My three sons! What a proud dad I am.

Domenick Raymond replied
I will always miss all the special times we shared and I cannot wait to see you again in Heaven pain free!! I love you Dad with all my heart!!! I feel you in my heart so I will always have you with me!! You will always be with me!!

Say hello to everyone in Heaven for me and keep singing the praises of Jesus for eternity!!! I LOVE YOU POPS!!!! I love you so very much!

Nicky replied
That was beautiful!

Will Always Be # 2

Daddy's
Pride & Joy

ENLIGHTEN

ENRICH

ENCOURAGE

GO YE MINISTRIES
IN THE WILDERNESS

MINISTRY

Family

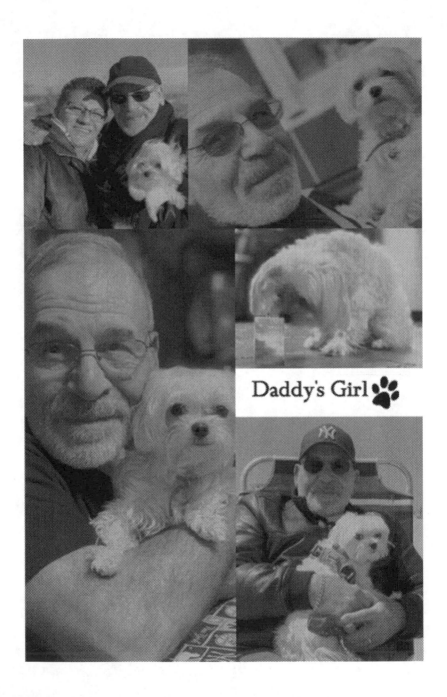

Daddy's Girl 🐾

Grandpa's

Blessings

These Are A
Few Of My

Favorite Things

His Passions And Talents

BIBLE
QUIZ

YANKEES

NICKY MOZZARELLA

57

I Love You Nicky

I was holding back the tears as I sat in the dentist chair waiting for my last filling before the dental insurance would end. It took three needles to numb the area to be filled. All I could think of was Nicky, picturing him in my mind as he always sat in the dentist's chair and watched as I was worked on in past visits. Knowing I was not a fan of the dentist, he would be praying for me with a smile of admiration on his face every single visit. (But he wasn't there!) He would take a few pictures without me knowing and share them on our family text. (But he wasn't there!) After it was all over and sitting in our car, he would hold my hand with these words, "I'm proud of you." (But he wasn't there!) It was a hard day for me without him to support me with a prayer and his smile and no one to hold my hand with such love. (He just wasn't there.)

With a heavy heart I took a drive to where it all began - Silver Lake. First stop was the gas station where he had worked. I reminisced of the times we sat in the car talking of how much we loved each other. (And we kissed.) Second stop was the old building which once was "The Italian Club" where we would be every weekend to dance, and yes we were drinking (blue flame was my drink of choice). It was a jigger that lit on fire and was downed in one shot followed by seven and seven. Those were the days before coming to the saving knowledge of Jesus Christ. Night after night Nicky would sing with the group appearing. He sang with famous groups who were always amazed at the smoothness and quality of his voice. I was proud every single time as he would stand up there and sing ... he was my date. He'd usher me onto the dance floor where I always had two left feet, but he would move his legs just as smooth as he could sing. What a dancer he was! I was proud of how everyone knew him, everywhere we went he knew somebody and was very well liked. He was a sharp dresser and didn't like a hair out of place. He was known as "Nicky Boy" and later as "Nicky Norker."

I continued on down the street where we first met. That was the night I was breaking up with my boyfriend, Anthony, and he walked in the door asking me for a date. Odd as it may seem, it was the beginning.

Continuing to drive I went to our first home ... we had three amazing baby boys while living in that home. Second floor and down to the first because we needed more room for our third son to love. We were so in love yet there was that raging fire within. We had good times in that house. It was not just a house but our home.

I drove around the neighborhood where it all began. Reminiscing of how young we were – just two kids. It was an emotional drive and one I needed as a part of this journey that only God could get me through.

I often find myself during the day exclaiming these words out loud, "I love you Nicky!" Although he is no longer with me here on this planet, he will always live in my heart. In the midst of all the ups and downs there were times, many times when we would stop in the kitchen or whatever room we were in and just hug. We held onto each other for a long time and could feel the love like liquid gold flow from each other as we would express our love. Our boys didn't see that as the days went by, but we loved each other deeply. There were nights we would sit in our recliners and in the midst of the what we were watching, just look at each other and smile (especially when watching our son preach). He'd grab my hand and tell me how God was so good to us and how he loved me. There were many times while driving, whether singing or not, just randomly holding hands like it was nobody's business. We fought with a passion but loved with that same passion.

This past summer of 2020 (September 13, five months before his passing) he sang on our deck using his big black speaker on wheels that his children had given him. How happy he was as he sang as if the trees were soaking it all in. I watched with admiration and joined in, but the best part was when he took my hand and we danced. Everyone else was in the house but he didn't care. We held each other and danced like we were kids. This was the heart of my husband. Forever I will be saying, "I LOVE YOU NICKY!" I was sixteen when we met and have been with him for forty-eight years. He was the only man I have ever loved. Forever I will whisper, "I love you Nicky." I always loved him, I love him now and will forever love him. My heart will whisper on, "I love you Nicky."

I Don't Want To!

No matter where or in whom my faith lies, this is a path I do NOT want to take. It's a hard path and I don't want to! I don't want to live my life without him! I don't want to live alone! And I certainly don't EVER want to be labeled a widow! I am young and alive and very much driven by a Call of God upon my life, but all the particulars in between? I don't want to! I don't want to do it!

This is a part of life that we have no control over. It is something that causes grief and great sorrow that we have no control over. We cannot change anything even though we would like to. Death is a fact of life that we must accept no matter what, but truth be told - I don't want to! I have never been a child who kicked and screamed. I had to buck up and accept whatever came my way, but this time I want to cry. I want to stomp my foot and say make it go away, stop this now, however it will change nothing.

I see Nicky's face everywhere. To sit on the recliner and watch a movie is like a nightmare because he is not sitting to my left. The song playing in the supermarket reminds me that if he were with me he'd be singing it. Driving down the highway that we took thousands of time together, our favorite spots we'd like to go and eat, just the two of us - we had our special spots and now he is not with me to go and I am alone. I am alone … I don't want to! I don't want to do this!

As childish as this may seem and unexpected from "your

evangelist for such a time as this," it is what it is. My life has changed and I don't want it to. Let me explain some things:

It's ok to cry. It's ok to say you don't want to. It's ok to be filled with grief and sorrow. It's ok to want to wake up from this bad dream, this nightmare - it's ok. What's not ok is living there and I know it. *I am allowing my feelings to run their course with an expectancy from my Heavenly Father to hold me through the process.*

Grief is as much a part of life as is sorrow, disappointments, anger and fear of the unknown. This is all God given emotions for a time and a season, but we are not to camp out or live in that season. Although I am experiencing it, I also know it has to run its course. If you have lost a loved one or are facing the possibility of knowing it is coming, I would like to share my experience along this journey in hopes that it may be of some comfort to you now or in the coming days.

My Story ...

Being a public figure with thousands standing in the gap for my husband in prayer, I knew I had to appear publicly with the news. As devastating as it was, two hours after being informed of his passing I appeared on Facebook with it. In addition to the information I also made the statement that I did not want to talk on the phone or text, etc. THANK YOU to all those who have respected that! In a time like this I realize many want to call with concern, love and support but I did not want to talk to anyone. I was just there. I felt like I was suspended in time and only existed. I wanted to sit alone and cry. It's ok to cry.

In addition my family gathered around me like glue, each one hugging and caring for me, not wanting to leave me alone for a moment. My boys asking through tears, "are you ok?" We spent hours at our kitchen table talking, crying, laughing and crying some more. It was hard but it was a beautiful hard. This went on for days. I still received calls and texts and read every text and listened to every phone call, however I did not respond. I was suspended in mere existence.

I was blessed to be surrounded every single day for two weeks by my entire family, twelve of us together just loving each other with the support of our presence. It was the hardest yet the greatest time of my life. We were all under one roof, no matter how sloppy the house was or tight and inconvenient, no one minded. We were all together. The love we drew from each other was beautiful. The closeness bonded us greater than ever before. We are a FAMILY.

I want you to know that in the midst of all this love, support and togetherness I spent much time sneaking away to scream into the towel. I have ached like never before, cried and moaned in PAIN like never before. It became a habit to engulf my face within a towel so no one would hear me and LET IT ALL OUT! I MISSED MY HUSBAND AND I WANTED HIM BACK!

Let me suggest to you;

- It is ok to let it go ... be upset and hurt ... it's ok.
- Take the time to cry, reminisce and face the sorrow within. It is hard but I have found it to be necessary for healing.
- It's ok to mourn. Don't avoid the memories of your loved one. As hard as it is, it is part of the healing. Don't avoid it.
- It's ok not to want to talk to anyone ... be yourself. Your life has changed forever and it's ok to take time with yourself.
- Don't run from your feelings – face them and let it hurt ... it's a healing process.
- Talk to God and let Him hold you in His arms. Feel His Presence and weep on Him ... it's ok.
- Be assured ... know within yourself that this is a process, you will get through this.
- If you do not face your feelings and process the time as it comes, it will return at a later time with a greater grief.

How can I speak with experience as I have only recently experienced this loss? Because I know the Voice of my Heavenly Father and it is He who has directed me to move forward with this book. These are some things I'd like to share:

With God all things are possible.

With Him you are never alone.

With His help we WILL make it!

You may be saying that you don't have a family to surround you. You may be carrying the load of younger children or concerns of the unknown. You may be alone to carry the burden but please hear me out.

Throughout the time of my husband's illness, as soon as I asked for prayer from God's children, I began to experience a peace that I cannot explain. I had a strength and it felt as if I was being carried. I knew I was undergirded, someone was lifting me and carrying me physically to the point that I thought I was heartless and something was wrong with me.

From the day I surrendered my life to Jesus and invited Him to be my Lord and Savior I have been a part of the family of God. I felt the prayers! I tangibly, physically felt the prayers of my church family. I KNOW they were praying and God was answering - I know it! My family and I were receiving food daily from people all over who cared. We received such love that my heart cried to overflowing. My church family was there for us, people from other churches, cards, letters, texts, phone calls, messages from people in different parts of the world. The support system was huge and ever so appreciated. I felt every prayer and every bit of the support.

1. *If you are without a home church you are missing out on a great family.* You may be asking why are they a family if

no one reached out to my husband when he needed them to? Let me explain that it is easier to treat something you can see. A physical wound can be bandaged, but a mental wound is hard to detect and I believe *it's time for us all to be educated on how to deal with it.* The brain is as much a part of the body as a limb. There has been a stigma on mental illness but the brain is just another part of the body as is a hand or a foot. If there is a wound in the brain then it needs to be treated so it can heal. People perish for lack of knowledge, *it's time we educate ourselves on how to deal with and help those suffering (and it is suffering) with mental illness.*

2. ***Unless your life is surrendered to Jesus and turned around to live for Him, you will not have a support system or real peace.*** Each prayer that went up on my behalf was felt. I believe that all the prayers collectively have built an undergirding that has carried me and surrounded me with wings of angels. I can feel them, no matter what I have been going through. Fear has never passed through my heart for one single moment. There has been a great peace that I cannot explain. My heart is sad, very sad as I love my husband and will miss him and the personal things we shared together but peace has flooded my very being. Knowing Jesus and knowing I have a church family as a support system is like nothing that can be compared. *You need Jesus to make it.*

3. **Hide God's Word in your heart.** During the entire experience with my husband's sickness my heart, mind and life was dedicated to making sure he got better. Seeing what he was going through, hearing it in his voice, seeing his weakness and not even once being able to see him while in the hospital. It was the longest nightmare I have ever been through. Although I was not with him physically in the hospital I was with him every moment of every day in my very being. He was all that was on my mind ... constantly.

I could not pick up my Bible or devotional for almost two months. I felt like I was just "there". I was awake but not alive ... just there. I went from reading my Bible every single day of my life to not a single word. It wasn't in me ... I couldn't do it. It bothered me more than anything that I was not even picking up the Book. I did not even want to read it, I just wanted to breathe. I just wanted to walk, talk and exist by breathing. That is exactly how I felt. I would sit up in bed and be empty ... just there. No thoughts, no worries, no nothing ... just there. I did not want to be around anyone or talk to anyone or cook, clean or even play with my grandchildren (and that's not me). I just wanted to be suspended like I was hovering over the world. I was there but not ... I was just there. (This may not be making any sense to you, maybe it does, but it is the best way I can explain it). Not opening my Bible let me realize I was not myself and something was off. After sharing this to a friend in a text she told me not to worry about it because I have read God's Word and it is in my heart. She said that through the years God has planted His Word in my heart and I can ask the Holy Spirit to bring to memory what is stored up in my mind, what I need in crisis time. This released me! (Thank you, Mary Ann Colletti). It was all those years of daily reading my Bible that brought His Word Alive WHEN I NEEDED IT. I rest upon His Word and you will too.

Most Importantly

God has a plan and a purpose for everything

Please do not be angry at God. *God has a plan and a purpose for everything.* If you pray and the answer is not what you expected, there is a reason and God knows best.

This past year my husband was diagnosed with Lymphoma. During a biopsy done on the left side of his groin his nerve was damaged, so in addition to all he was going through he had to endure the damaged nerve. This left him with the feeling of his entire left leg being asleep all the time. It was additional pain that was tormenting him as there was no relief. It became infected and the leg swelled to one size from the thigh down and changed in color, like a burgundy. It was infected, so in addition to treatments for the cancer he was also treated for this ongoing infection. God knows what He is doing.

I believe my Heavenly Father did answer our prayers in His way and in His time and I'm ok with that. I believe He saved my husband from what could have been a long road ahead with the cancer as well as the damaged nerve in his leg. I believe he did get his miracle. He no longer has pain! He no longer or will ever feel the feelings of rejection! He no longer or ever will feel lonely or misunderstood! He no longer has to limp or try to hide when bending because he doesn't want anyone to see that he can't do it anymore … He can! He no longer has stiff hands that won't open or close! I believe God gave my husband the ultimate healing and in His mercy gave him the alone time in the hospital to heal his heart and soul first.

Please don't be angry at God because *God has a plan and a purpose for everything.* In addition to carrying your loved one in glory He will carry you and I just as well if we trust Him.

- Surround yourself with the family of God
- Be a part of a church as they will be your support system

Not my will but thine

I have gone through "roughly" 2,756 messages and read every single one on Facebook, over 150 inbox messages and 240 cards and letters as of this writing. There have been hundreds of phone calls and texts and I personally have heard from a list of countries: Africa, Australia, Brazil, Canada, Dubai, Ecuador, France, Guiana, Hungary, Italy, Norway, Puerto Rico, Scotland, Spain and all over the United States. Words can NOT express the love I feel in my heart! I want to THANK every single one who took of your time and expressed your concern for my family and I. This is overwhelming in a good way. THANK YOU EVERYONE!

There was a live appearance on Facebook sharing the news of my husband's passing that had over eight thousand views. My point is that through what is a very sad time for my family and I has turned into an open door of opportunity to share the gospel of Jesus Christ in "living form." Did I mention that the very next day, after my husband's passing, I was notified of two people surrendering their hearts to Jesus?

It's one thing to hear about the gospel but another to see it lived out. I am not saying this in a braggadocious manner but hear my heart. Through this time God has touched people in ways that I could never have done. He has allowed thousands to not only hear of the gospel of Jesus but SEE Him and His Word in action.

How many apples will grow from a single seed? Only God knows the answer to that question. Well, let me ask you … if someone's life is affected by the gospel of Jesus Christ, how many others will be affected through that one? I was the only one in my entire family to accept Jesus and it was not easy, but today only God knows how many have been affected. If souls are getting saved in another country, how many will that one soul reach? Can you see it? To infinity and beyond!

Although death is hard, and it is, *it is imperative to come to grips with the fact that God must have His way as He has a plan that far surpasses anything we can ever ask or think.* In loving my Heavenly Father I must be willing to say not my will but Yours Lord and trust Him to take care of my family and I and everything else, In Jesus' Name.

THANK YOU!

I want to personally thank every single person who has sent cards, flowers, plants, gift baskets, trinkets and gifts. Thank you!

I want to thank every person who took the time to cook for my family or order our best meals. Thank you!

I want to thank every person who took the time to text and call and even those who I know it was difficult not to call and didn't. I appreciate every single one of you, Thank you!

I want to thank my church family, near and far. If it weren't for your prayers, love and concern I would not be able to stand right now. You have supported my family and I by laying us at the cross of Jesus and it is He who has carried us. Thank you!

I want to thank God for my family as Lord, You gave me the BEST! My sons, daughters in law, grandchildren … Lord … THANK YOU!!!

I want to thank YOU for purchasing this book as it shows that you are not defeated and will not give in to your feelings. In light of all you are going through, may it be the loss of your soul mate, dealing with depression or knowing you are about to face something you are not ready for and just don't want to, just the fact that you have this book in your hand says you want help. You don't want to go it alone and want to know how to make it through the most difficult journey of your life. You want to make it to the next day. You want to be there for your children, you want to live. You want to be able to breathe without hurting or see his or her face and not fall apart. Or maybe you're living with someone in pain, physical, or emotional pain and you just don't know how to deal with it any longer. Hopefully this book has brought some relief in knowing it is real and you are not alone. Hopefully it has brought an awareness of why someone acts or reacts the way they do and it's not a direct attack against you. You WILL make it! Give yourself a bit of time and know that with God's help YOU WILL MAKE IT!

A Field Trip to Heaven

Last but not least:

"I wonder what grandpa saw when he woke up in heaven?" were the words our grandson, Zachary, asked upon hearing of grandpa's passing.

Hmmm ... I wonder

Our grandson, Gideon, said; "He's gonna see King David! and his wife!"

Welcomed home by our loving master ... I can only imagine - will we sing or will we dance?

I don't have the answer for anyone but one thing I do know for sure is there will be no more sorrow, no more pain, no more doubt and much more to gain.

It will be warm and lit up by the light of our master, a light we cannot describe here on earth. The jewels: diamonds, rubies, emeralds and pearls, streets of gold and the softness of His Presence. There will be songs of praise upon each lip and angel's wings to wave His praise. Can you see it? No more sorrow, no more pain. We will be loved by everyone and we too will love all - in a way our human mind cannot understand. Such love, an unconditional love - a love that will come from our Heavenly Father God and our Lord and Savior Jesus Christ and won't it be amazing?

If we ever had the opportunity to take a field trip to heaven I'm sure it would be a place where we would never want to leave. It would be grander and more majestic than words can describe. Never alone, no never alone - a place with belonging, each to everyone and our God alone.

Oh ... If we could take a field trip to heaven.

Don't mourn, one day as we live for Jesus here on earth we will one day live WITH Him in Glory. HALLELUJAH!!! THANK YOU JESUS!!! THANK YOU FOR MAKING A WAY FOR US!!!

Scripture References

John 3:16 *(NKJV)*
For God so loved the world that He gave His only begotten Son, that whoever believes in Him should not perish but have everlasting life.

2 Chronicles 7:14 *(NKJV)*
If My people who are called by My name will humble themselves, and pray and seek My face, and turn from their wicked ways, then I will hear from heaven, and will forgive their sin and heal their land.

2 Timothy 1:7 *(NKJV)*
For God has not given us a spirit of fear, but of power and of love and of a sound mind

Hebrews 8:12 *(NKJV)*
For I will be merciful to their unrighteousness, and their sins and their lawless deeds I will remember no more."

1 Thessalonians 4:17 *(NKJV)*
Then we who are alive and remain shall be caught up together with them in the clouds to meet the Lord in the air. And thus we shall always be with the Lord.

1 Corinthians 15:55-57 *(KJV)*
O death, where is thy sting? O grave, where is thy victory? The sting of death is sin; and the strength of sin is the law. But thanks be to God, which giveth us the victory through our Lord Jesus Christ.

2 Corinthians 4:17-18 *(NKJV)*
For our light affliction, which is but for a moment, is working for us a far more exceeding and eternal weight of glory, while we do not look at the things which are seen, but at the things which are not seen. For the things which are seen are temporary, but the things which are not seen are eternal.

2 Corinthians 1:3-4 *(NKJV)*
Blessed be the God and Father of our Lord Jesus Christ, the Father of mercies and God of all comfort, who comforts us in all our tribulation, that we may be able to comfort those who are in any trouble, with the comfort with which we ourselves are comforted by God.

Psalm 27:14 *(NKJV)*
Wait on the Lord; Be of good courage, And He shall strengthen your heart; Wait, I say, on the Lord!

Matthew 5:4 *(NKJV)*
Blessed are those who mourn, For they shall be comforted.

Isaiah 26:3 *(NKJV)*
You will keep him in perfect peace, Whose mind is stayed on You, Because he trusts in You.

Joshua 1:9 *(NKJV)*
Have I not commanded you? Be strong and of good courage; do not be afraid, nor be dismayed, for the Lord your God is with you wherever you go."

Tribute to a Great Man

Nick's Legacy

Good Morning! Mary and I are so sorry we cannot be with all of you this morning as you celebrate Nick's life. We too want to celebrate him!! Nick contributed a lot to our lives as well as to the ministry of Full Gospel Church.

Looking back over the 30 plus years we have known Nick, we have seen God use him to encourage others and to further the Gospel. Nick always was willing to help, no task too small. From driving the church van to coaching the Bible Quiz teams, from running the audio equipment to singing in the choir, from cooking for our staff breakfast to manning the hot dog truck at our Harvestfest, to whipping up a batch of mozzarella, he was always willing to serve.

We were always touched when Nick would be praying with someone at the altar, or sharing a song from his heart.

God tells us He gives good gifts to his children, and Nick was a good gift to us! To his family, we say thank you for sharing him with us.

Pastor Ronald DePasquale, Livingston Full Gospel Church

12/21/1949
-
2/2/2021

It's You Lord

(Prayer for the World)
By: Domenick Raymond DiBenedetto
(2-14-03 - revised 7.1.20)

When I look around me
All I see is pain
When I look around me
I feel the need to call your name
Cause' the world is lost
On the road of no return
Lord use my life as a living light
To make their hearts somehow turn

To you Lord, to you Lord
With your arms open wide
From you Lord, from you Lord
Let them know that they can't hide
From your holy presence
From your awesome love
Lord show this world
Without you they can't survive

In this world so cold and lonely
I see people everyday

Jean Ann DiBenedetto

Searching for the answers
To the problems that they face
Giving no thought of you
The only one who can help them through
Lord use my life as a living light
To make them somehow learn that

It's you Lord, it's you Lord
With your arms open wide
From you Lord, from you Lord
Let them know that they can't hide
From your holy presence
From your awesome love
Lord show this world
Without you they can't survive

Lord make yourself real
To this lonely world
Please show them that you
their problems can heal
Let them know without you
They'll never make it through
Show them your plan
Is to hold them in your hand

To you Lord, it's you Lord
With your arms open wide
From you Lord, from you Lord
Let them know that they can't hide
From your holy presence
From your awesome love
Lord show this world
Without you they can't survive

To you Lord, it's you Lord
With your arms open wide
From you Lord, from you Lord
Let them know that they can't hide
From your holy presence
From your awesome love
Lord show this world
Without you they can't survive

Lord show this world,
They need you to feel alive[1]

[1]2003 Domenick Raymond DiBenedetto, *It'sYou Lord (Prayer for the World)*, All rights reserved by composer. Used by permission.

Military Honors

What Do I Do With The Grief?

So it's been two months since the passing of my husband and I have been asked how I am dealing with it. Let me give you a bird's eye view of grief.

It's the devil in disguise … he's not coming home. His clothes are hanging in the closet, there are drawers with clothes inside, his shoes, and his Apple Watch with the current time on it.

His cell phone is still plugged in next to my desk. His watch is there … it's just there. I don't want anyone to touch his watch … he loved his watch, it was from his son Domenick Raymond. He loved that watch. I can't part with it. His gold bracelet … I gave that to him about thirty years ago … he loved that bracelet. I don't want anyone to touch it. His songs are on his cell phone. His scent is in our bed. Can I hold onto the pillow? His picture is on my desk, hanging on the wall, on the refrigerator, in my Bible. I want to see his face! It hurts to see his smile and not be able to touch him. What do I do with this grief?

I find myself in a house with people, yet all alone. There is no one to talk to at the table, to watch a movie with and not be on a timeclock or an agenda. There is Valentine's Day, couples dinners … but I'm not a couple. Dinner with friends … but I'm alone. Coming home late at night to a house without a home … he WAS home. He put the lights on when I was coming home in the dark, he often met me at the door outside and carried my things, even if he was in a robe because of the late hour. No one is there to meet me at the door.

Sunday Morning, he'd make me hot water with a teaspoon of honey to soothe my throat. He's not here anymore … there's no one to make the hot water. "TEN MINUTES!" He'd shout just before time for me to hop on Facebook Ministry Live … "FIVE MINUTES!" "FOUR … THREE … TWO … ONE MINUTE!" He'd shout with a smile … There's no countdown. He'd sit in the living room watching on his phone or sneak up where I did not see him and take a picture of me ministering. "That was GREAT!" He'd shout with exuberance when it ended. "I'm SO proud of you!" Almost always exclaiming after the last amen. There's no cheering section anymore … I'm on my own. "Jean Ann, you are their evangelist for such a time as this. No one preaches like you anymore," would be his sentiments time after time. "I love you Jean Ann" or "I love you Babe." No one to say I love you Babe. What do I do with this?

I'll tell you what I do with it:

- I drive down the highway and SCREAM out in PAIN!
- I CRY out … I LOVE YOU NICKY!
- I talk to him knowing he's not here.
- I lay in bed at night asking God to please tell my husband that I love him.
- I cry in such agony that no one can understand.
- Some days I'm so weak I just don't want to get out of bed.

I understand that things are never going to be the same for me again, but I've got to tell you that I KNOW that. And knowing that is hard enough, but trying to hold onto the mourning of it would be disastrous. I cannot or will not do it. I **have** a hope and a future ahead and I must follow my Heavenly Father to taste of it. I have told myself that I can NOT live in that state of being.

Yes, I believe it's ok to cry, shout, scream, do whatever it takes to get it all out. I do believe it is ok to smell his clothes or gaze into the mirror with him in the shadow. I do believe it's ok to talk to my husband … the only lover I have ever had. I do believe it is not only ok, but that it is necessary. It is necessary to let it out. It must be released or it will fester and grow like a mold that will be harmful for everyone in contact.

My Strength –

I have found that being with people that I know care about me has given me an invisible strength. I have visited a church just to be near people that I know love me. To just sit in the pew was enough. Although many came around me, all I needed was to be there. Just having lunch with girlfriends (even if we haven't conversed in ages) helps. I need to be with people. I try to surround myself with those that wrap their arms around me and are not afraid to cry with me or tell me that they love me. I need that. I need to see people's faces. I've got to talk to people. This gives me an invisible strength that I need at this time to make it through this journey and make it I will.

I have found that getting out of my house has been good for me. It's not good to be alone or stay within the same environment day after day. It can get old and even when you don't think so it reveals itself in other ways. If we want to be free we must get out and be with someone. We've got to get out of our shell or we will die just like the lobster that has to shed his skin. If he is not willing to hit against the rocks under the ocean he will suffocate within his shell. If we stay within the safety of our quarters it will one day prove to be a "false" safety. We've got to surround ourselves with believers. It is a necessary addition to life and breath.

Jesus came for people, if we avoid being with people we develop a false sense of security and eventually become unable to feel secure around anyone other than our walls. This brings captivity – held captive by our fears, even if that is fear of people. Fear of opening up and letting anyone into your life. It is a necessary part of life as Jesus is our ultimate example and He let those He trusted into His life right up until death. Life becomes a secret without the ability to allow anyone in. Some would say it becomes a disorder as it is not the norm.

In all the grief it is an easy solution to be alone and hurt. The pain of loss and loneliness will grow like ivy on the side of a building and before long it will cover the entire view. If we live in the pain it will offset the view of reality. We've got to face reality.

No, my husband is not coming home. No, he will not be in our bed. No, he is not going to sit at the table with me at dinner time. No, he is not going to sit and watch a movie with me. No … nothing is ever going to be the same as it was ever again. So what do I do with it now? Do I wallow in the past? Do I mourn over the loss? Do I live in the pain? There must be a way to deal with it and be free.

Freedom is in our Lord God Almighty. What do I do? I sit in His Presence and let Him wrap His arms around me. Without words I allow Him to breathe life into my being, a peace that words cannot describe. I speak to Him as if He is sitting on my bed with me or in my car or even at my kitchen table. He hears my sigh. He holds my hand when I am hurting … I know it.

What you don't know is prior to the loss of my own husband he and I had been experiencing a loss for one year prior that we had shed many tears over. We carried the loss in our hearts and the pain with our hands tied while watching deception at its finest and Satan having a field day. It was unbearable as we watched for three years something that led to one of the greatest hurts we could have ever imagined. It was a fight to keep sane in the face of daily depression.

Of course the unexpected and even shocking passing of my husband came with great grief. Now I carry alone the pain of grief number one and grief number two. In addition to being in the midst of all the grief was another situation that caused more pain than I can explain. Grief number three … It causes sleepless nights, eating uncontrollably, tears of sorrow, disappointment, worry and physical pain. I was experiencing pain in my chest that oftentimes would hurt to breathe and pain in my stomach that took some doing to keep it all down. I developed a rash on the back of my neck and itching on my body, which was all due to the STRESS, the HURT that not one person in this world could understand and even realize why it hurt me so badly. People will never know because there is no way for me to even explain, but the PAIN of the GRIEF and the LOSS was and still is without words. It is enough to drive someone to medication or a doctor's care but you see it is not. What it is driving me to do is to hold onto the hem of my Savior's garment. You see, I am the woman with the issue of blood. I am bleeding on the inside and it HURTS … my head, heart, stomach, and limbs … but the worst is my spirit. Satan has worked overtime to crush my spirit but HOW DARE he!

I will NOT let the enemy of my soul have a foot hold in my life! I have fought and tried too hard to be a woman of integrity and strive to be of stellar character. I fall short constantly, but I will not stop striving. Over my dead body will I allow the enemy of my soul to take away all the years of grasping for the freedom and liberty that comes from my Heavenly Father. I will NOT give in to the enemy's tactics and allow him to drive me into a deep depression of sorrow, grief and worry. It will NOT happen!

You see that is where you and I need to be in times of great and exhausting trials, situations that can suck the life out of us. We must make up our minds that no matter what we are going through we will NOT allow Satan an entrance into our mind. You see he starts with thoughts, then feelings and before you know it we have lost strength because we have lost hope. I will NOT let him do it to me!!!

There are ways I have drawn strength. I cling to the horns of the altar. Every single morning and night I talk to my God. I don't care if it's in tears or words of my heart, I have a conversation with Him. I hold onto Him, before I close my eyes at night and the moment they open in the morning. He is the first and last person I speak to every single day of my life. I NEED Him and NEED to KNOW that He hears my every cry. I pray for others and it takes away the "me". My focus could be on me, but if I am speaking to my Heavenly Father on behalf of someone in need the focus is off me and my problems. I don't miss church. I NEED to be in the HOUSE OF GOD. It's not enough to join in online, but I NEED to see people's faces and hear the voices of worship and sit in God's Presence. I NEED to feel the joy and expectancy of paying my tithes … it's so much fun. I NEED that. I NEED to know that people care about me. I have never been like this in my life but I am now. I NEED to know you care. It speaks to me and feeds me when I hear kind words and words of love and affirmation … I NEED that right now in this time of my life. You will not have your full freedom and deliverance from grief if you withhold your worship, fellowship and tithes. It is all part of deliverance as obedience brings freedom.

I still cry, but I don't MOURN. Even at times when it's even hard to open my Bible, I speak to my Heavenly Father and ask Him to speak to me. I am in the beginnings of jumping full force back into full time ministry as my Heavenly Father has directed me. Although I was fearful at first to bring the Word, as I felt I was not giving my best, I was set free as soon as I stood on the platform for the first time since my husband's home-going.

I am walking a journey and I'd be a fool to think it is over, but one thing I know for sure is that through the prayers of my brethren, He has been holding me up in times I could not stand. He has wrapped His arms around me when I could not bear it alone and He has breathed His breath of life into my lungs when my chest was bruised with sorrow and grief.

I talk to Him constantly, fill my home with worship to invite God's Presence, not loud praises but music to bring me to the throne. I go to the altar of my heart and lay it before my King. He knows the pain and sorrow and my faith is in Him to know that He will soothe my heart and calm all my fears.

I have served the devil notice and told him that no matter what people have said to me about the expected sorrow to come, I will not have it. I have come to grips from day one that my husband is in no more pain and that he is whole. He has a new body with strong legs and a smile on his oh so handsome face and one day I will see him and we will hold each other in our arms and rejoice together in the Presence of our King. I have that hope and although I grasp for something more to tell you as how I deal with this there is none. My hope is in Jesus and I know that as long as I do my part He will do His. I don't have to curl up and die if I give it all to Him. I am trusting Him with my life every single day. I am thinking differently and making choices with great thought.

True, I have not been myself and yes I am in a funk as I continue to face daily the grief of three different situations in my life beyond my control, but one thing I have come to grips with is this: I may not know what holds tomorrow but I KNOW Who holds my hand. And … Because He (my God) lives I live. It's in Him that I live and move and have my being.

I am not myself and very sensitive right now, but I have learned that if I have to cry just do it. If I have to be alone, just do it. If I have to face sorrow just do it, but one thing I have never faced and that's anger.

I have never been angry at my Heavenly Father over the loss of my husband or any one of the situations I am facing. There is a devil that people allow to make decisions for them, and unfortunately their decisions at times do affect the ones who love them most, but God is still on the throne. There is no one who has the authority to move God off the throne as He is the same yesterday, today and forever. He was a miracle in biblical time, He's still a miracle today and will be a miracle worker tomorrow. If I didn't get my miracle yesterday I may get it today, if I don't get my miracle today, I may get it tomorrow. I will always have a hope. My hope is in my Heavenly

Father, His Son Jesus and the Holy Spirit to empower me to make it day by day.

I pray In Jesus' Name that you will allow yourself the privilege to surrender yourself, your baggage and all your grief, pain and sorrow to our God Almighty. Jesus went to the cross for you, in your place. Ask Him for forgiveness and believe that He died on the cross for you and accept Him now, and then you will be on your way to a journey of Life. He rose from the dead and because He lives you now can live also. Let God give you New Life, so that you may never ever walk around again being Shattered.

Six months later ...

It has been six months and I'm still going strong. There are times when I cry like a baby because I realize now that I lost my best friend and he was all I had. I still have not given his clothes away solely because I want to give them to someone who will use them. His phone is disconnected but still sits on the charger. I don't know why but it just is. I keep his picture on my desk where I work all day – I just love to see his face. What I miss most is looking into his eyes. I can remember times when we just looked into each other's eyes and cried because we loved each other so much (little secrets no one needed to know). I still don't like to sit in my living room alone as he was always on the recliner next to me. There are movies I cannot see me watching because they were with him and it's just not the same. One of the things that I am shocked about is that cooking was always a passion of mine and now I can't stand it. I realize I cooked because he enjoyed it so much and now there's just no reason. I do not want to cook.

Fourth of July was very difficult for me this year because when I was at my sister's house I could envision him everywhere. I saw where he was sitting, in his tan shorts and white polo shirt with the American flag and sporting that white Polo hat, it was very difficult for me. I left early and knowing I was returning home alone my mind was wandering. I realized just in time that there was a truck in front of me. I found myself driving on the opposite side of the road and getting into bed while it was still light out and feeling sick to my stomach and very much alone.

Since music was such a big part of our lives (there are two songs that he used to sing to me all the time) I feel that if I can make it through those songs without breaking down I have made it over a big hurdle. The two songs are: *I Do Love You* by Billy Stewart and the other is *So In Love* sung by the Tymes. In past months I would wail uncontrollably when I would put one on, but I am deliberately listening to them when I am alone in the car because I feel that is something I must accomplish. It is getting better.

I've gone back into ministry, however I'm taking it at a more relaxed pace. My heart is not aching as in past months, but one of the difficulties in the ministry is that we were always together. As an Evangelist I am in a different church most Sundays and that has been a challenge for me. Most churches have been places where we went together and this past Sunday I could envision Nicky and what he would do ... it was hard at first but God strengthened me and the service was great. Only God!

I have found it difficult even listening to Christian music as we did that together, we prayed together, read the Bible, discussed it, rejoiced together over God's goodness ... it has just been different. When I would go to a church without him he would take my hand and pray for me or if I was out of town he would call and pray – those are the little things I took for granted.

I am taking it slow and have great peace about it. I am still relying on the prayers of my Christian brothers and sisters because I don't want to face this alone just yet. I find great comfort in knowing that I am prayed for and especially love it when I receive texts, messages or phone calls from my sisters in Christ. Going to lunch and being together is like gas in the tank for me, it's a boost I cannot explain.

On the other hand, I must admit that I've got to overcome the sting of those who have not made much of an effort to check up on me. I thought it was self-pity but I have realized that I am seeing things I never wanted to see in times past. It's all becoming a reality to me and I believe my focus must not be on the negative but on Jesus and what my Heavenly Father has next on His agenda for me to do.

It took a while before I could get back into my daily Bible reading but I praise God that the desire is back and I am loving God's Word with a new hunger. In this time, I am noticing a keen discernment and more sensitivity to the spirit world than before. Some things I don't even want to know, but I believe the Lord is nudging me along to see through the fog, because there is something more important than anything in life and that is to be ready for the return of Jesus.

My call has been firing up and although the message is not always desirable, there is a fire inside of me to pursue forward in hopes that maybe it will cause someone to think. I'd like to be more like others, thinking it would make me a more likeable person, but that is not my calling. It's a hard one but doing what I know my Heavenly Father wants brings me peace.

In saying that – there will NEVER be a quick fix for grief, depression or loss, but I have found that as Solomon says; "all is vanity" that there is nothing greater in my life than hearing the Voice of my Heavenly Father and knowing that I am in His Will. I realize I am speaking as a minister here and maybe you are not, but your peace will still come the same. There is no quick fix but there is a process. I am finding that my process is diving into God's Word and talking to Him all the time … ALL the time. He's my world … my life … my best friend.

Your PEACE will come when you cry out to God and allow Him to take the sorrow and grief. Hold steady and wait until He calms your heart and soothes your pain … He WILL do it. No one can take away grief, mourning and pain like Jesus. He turns our mourning into dancing (as David exclaimed in *Psalm 30:11)*. In times when I am hit hard, I cry if I want to and let it go, then I cry some more ... it hurts! I then turn to God and tell Him how I am feeling. I know He wraps His arms around me because the hurt and pain dissipates and peace fills my inner most being. Hold onto your Heavenly Father. *If you don't know Him, you can, just by talking to Him in your own words and let Him carry you. Take it one day at a time but this time you are not alone.*

The hardest thing for me at this point is not hearing from people I would expect to hear from. However, time has passed and people move on and I need to as well. I'm sure as time goes on the cliché "out of sight, out of mind" rings true. I believe with human nature and busy schedules it is to be expected. I realize my life and maybe yours (if you have lost a loved one) will never be the same – we must guard our hearts and draw our strength from our relationship with our Heavenly Father. Hold onto the hem of His garment if you have to.

Within the past few weeks there are two messages that I had the privilege of preaching. I struggled with them as I thought they were just for me. I want to share my notes with you as I believe there is truth in God's Word and always Good News.

Message #1

SOLID FOUNDATION
How to make it in a world of disappointments.
What to do when things don't go the
way you expected or planned.

Throughout the years I have built a **solid foundation** that would keep me from falling in difficult times.

1. Diligently and DAILY **reading** and **studying** the Word of God.
    a. Building a Wall of Faith
        Ephesians 6:16 (NLT) *Hold up the shield of faith, to stop the fiery arrows of the devil.*
2. **Building a relationship** with my **Heavenly Father**.
    a. Prayer ... Communication with God ... just **talk** to Him.
3. Remembering how God has been there in the past.

These three steps are key.

Revelation 12:11 And they overcame him by the blood of the Lamb and by the word of their testimony.
WORD OF OUR TESTIMONY! Let the enemy know that you have a testimony ... tell him what it is. Speak to yourself so you know where the Lord has taken you from.

These are not steps in a Christian life that can be bypassed or overlooked. It is too important ... imperative to build a RELATIONSHIP with God!

Proverbs 18:10 "The name of the LORD is a strong tower: the righteous run into it, and are safe."

Tower –

Noun – it's a tall building or structure (so it's above the rest)

Verb – To rise or reach a great height.

Example: God TOWERS over everyone else.

YES HE DOES!!!!

1. So when we run to HIM – **HE SEES WHAT WE DON'T**
2. It's almost like He's our **lookout tower.**

- He protects us when we can't see what's ahead
- We feel **SAFE** and at **PEACE.**

My Peace is in my God because He knows my future and I don't.

We NEED to develop a SOLID FOUNDATION

1. Daily reading and studying God's Word creates a wall of faith that you can go to in times of trouble.
2. Build a relationship with your Heavenly Father by talking to Him daily. Don't just talk but wait to listen to His Still Small Voice.
3. Remember who He has been to you in times past. Know your testimony.

Building a Strong Foundation will help you to make it in a world of disappointments and know what to do when things don't go the way you expected or planned.

Message #2

The Rear View Mirror

Isaiah 43:18-19 (NKJ)

[18] *"Do not remember the former things, Nor consider the things of old.*
[19] *Behold, I will do a **new** thing, Now it shall spring forth; Shall you not*

know it? I will even make a road in the wilderness And rivers in the desert.

- We cannot look to our past or we will never see what God has for us in our future.

2 Corinthians 5:17 (NKJ)

*Therefore, if anyone is in Christ, he is a **new creation**; old things have passed away; behold, all things have become **new**.*

The purpose of a rear-view mirror

- To see who is behind you
- To see where you've been
- Sometimes there's a blind spot in your car and a rear-view mirror will help to see what you cannot otherwise see.

Aspects of the rear-view mirror

POSITIVE

We can't forget our past – where God brought us from.

1. Remember where He took us from
2. See who may be coming after you – sometimes there's an all too familiar thing going on and looking back we just might see something that brings us to.

NEGATIVE

1. We cannot hold onto the past.

2. We've got to get rid of the desires for our old lifestyle, good or bad. (change is hard) Married couples must learn to leave and cleave.

Jeremiah 29:11 (NKJ)
For I know the thoughts that I think toward you, says the Lord, thoughts of peace and not of evil, to give you a future and a hope.

A rear-view mirror is necessary but not to be a consistent habit. We've got to stop looking at what is behind us as it could cause an accident. Lord help us to not slow the process of where You want to take us. In Jesus' Name.

Shattered

The title of this book is *Shattered,* however it is a story not only of a woman who has lost her soulmate. It's not only a story of a person who was once whole and is now in two, but of a man who was shattered. He was a shattered man within himself all his life yet possessed something not everyone has. He had a love for his God and through all the brokenness and pain, emotionally and physically it was the Power of His Holy Spirit that enabled him to make it from day to day.

In the state in which my husband was encapsulated in pain, the pain of an overworked body breaking down on a consistent basis, as well as the pain of rejection and loneliness from everyone (including me at times) who did not understand the why. Why was he like that? Why? No ... it was easier to let distance be the force.

Living in such a state could have resulted in hospitalization, medication, addiction or even shutting down completely. However ... he lived a life that we now find out touched lives everywhere he went. I had no idea how many lives my husband touched. How did he do that? How did he work through the pain? How did he hold his head high without sleep for weeks? How did he laugh or sing when death of rejection and loneliness was knocking at the door of his heart? How did he make others feel like they were somebody?

You see even recently I was informed of a person who said that for some reason Nicky always had a special place in her heart because he always sat next to her and listened and made her feel like she was important. Someone at work said that she lost the father she never had. Coworkers asking who will pray for them now? Pastors and colleagues expressing to me now that they would have never known he was dealing with so much ... How can that be?

You see my husband was empowered by the Holy Spirit who gave him the strength to make it another day and not just make it but used him! My husband was "soul minded." He cared about people and loved people. He continued on day after day because there was a force that drove him and that was to provide for his wife, he had to do what he had to do. He continued on and ministerred in his own way to souls that no one would even give the time of day. My husband was a man that although seemed gruff and grouchy due to constant pain, was soul driven more than anything else. He would run for anyone who needed help and he did. He has driven miles to bless someone, gave until it hurt, cried in pain yet still labored to be of service many times. Although what seemed to be an inward person due to what was seen on the outward by those closest to him – he was in fact a very powerful Man of God driven by the Power of the Holy Spirit. You see it could only be the Holy Spirit that could have carried him right up until his very last breath.

The last words I heard him speak were, "Praise Jesus ... Praise Jesus ... Praise Jesus." On oxygen with barely breath to speak yet singing praises to his Heavenly Father ... how can that be? Because he was a man who loved his God. He pressed on shattered or not. You see, God used a man who was shattered all his life. It's not only me who is shattered due to my loss but he lived as a shattered man yet not many knew it. God can use even shattered vessels.

Please don't give up! You may think you are not able to do anything or ever be used by God because you too are shattered

... be it due to loss (like myself) or maybe living in that state like my beautiful husband. I want you to know that my husband is a testimony of how God can take a shattered person and still work through him and shine His love to others even through that brokneness. Your Heavenly Father is not through with you! Shattered is not a disability or a dead end with God. He can and will guide, love, direct and use you. Your life is not over! Surrender your sorrows, grief, disappointments and inadequacies to Jesus. He died on the cross for every single one of them. Do you think for one moment that the same Lord who sacrificed His life for you will ever leave you or tell you it's over? NO!

HE LOVES YOU AND IS HERE RIGHT NOW FOR YOU IF YOU WANT HIM. The Lord takes shattered vessels and turns them into priceless, matchless gems. My husband was a gem – shattered to many but a gem to his Heavenly Father. You too may be shattered but not to your Heavenly Father. Let Him have it all ... give him your shards ... every single one of them and let Him empower you to make it and leave a legacy.

Dedicated to a man who by The Power of the Holy Spirit left a legacy –

my husband ... Nicholas DiBenedetto Jr.

I always loved you, I love you still and always will. I love you Nicky!

About the author

Jean Ann is an evangelist for more than three decades throughout the US and abroad. She is a Wife, Mother and Nonna. She burns with the Fire of the Holy Spirit within her bringing life. Her delivery comes with laughter, tears and deep-down soul searching. The Love of Jesus is felt among all. Her ministry is fun yet fire, it touches the hardest heart and brings joy to the lowest soul. Jesus is her Lord and it is He who empowers her to bring life. Her exuberance will charm you to the edge of your seat culminating in transformation. You will laugh and cry but one thing for sure is you will never be the same again after hearing this powerful preacher. Jean Ann is familiar with all age groups, Retreats, Conferences, she's done it all ... but women and teens hold her heart as does Revival, it burns within her. Listeners experience Fun, Fire and Freedom.

Booking info:
Go Ye Ministries
Jean Ann DiBenedetto
PO Box 269
Hope, NJ 07844
info@goyeministries.com